Look and See ²

ACTIVITY BOOK

How old are you?	2
Unit 1: At School	4
Unit 2: Are You Happy?	10
Unit 3: Animals	16
Unit 4: Get Dressed	22
Unit 5: I Can Jump!	28
Unit 6: Faces	34
Unit 7: My Things	40
Unit 8: Babies	46
Unit 9: What's for Dinner?	52
Unit 10: Bugs	58
Berlitz Mid-Level Test	64
Berlitz End-of-Level Test	68
Language Booster	72

W0114874

NATIONAL GEOGRAPHIC LEARNING

Australia • Brazil • Mexico • Singapore • United Kingdom • United States

1 TR: 0.1 Listen, point, and say.

1

2

3

4

5

6

7

8

9

10

2 TR: 0.2 Listen and chant.

3 TR: 0.3 Listen, point, and say.

Aa **a**lligator

Ee **e**lephant

Ii **i**guana

Oo **o**ctopus

Uu **u**mbrellabird

1 Draw you. Say.

At School

1 TR: 1.1 Listen and circle.

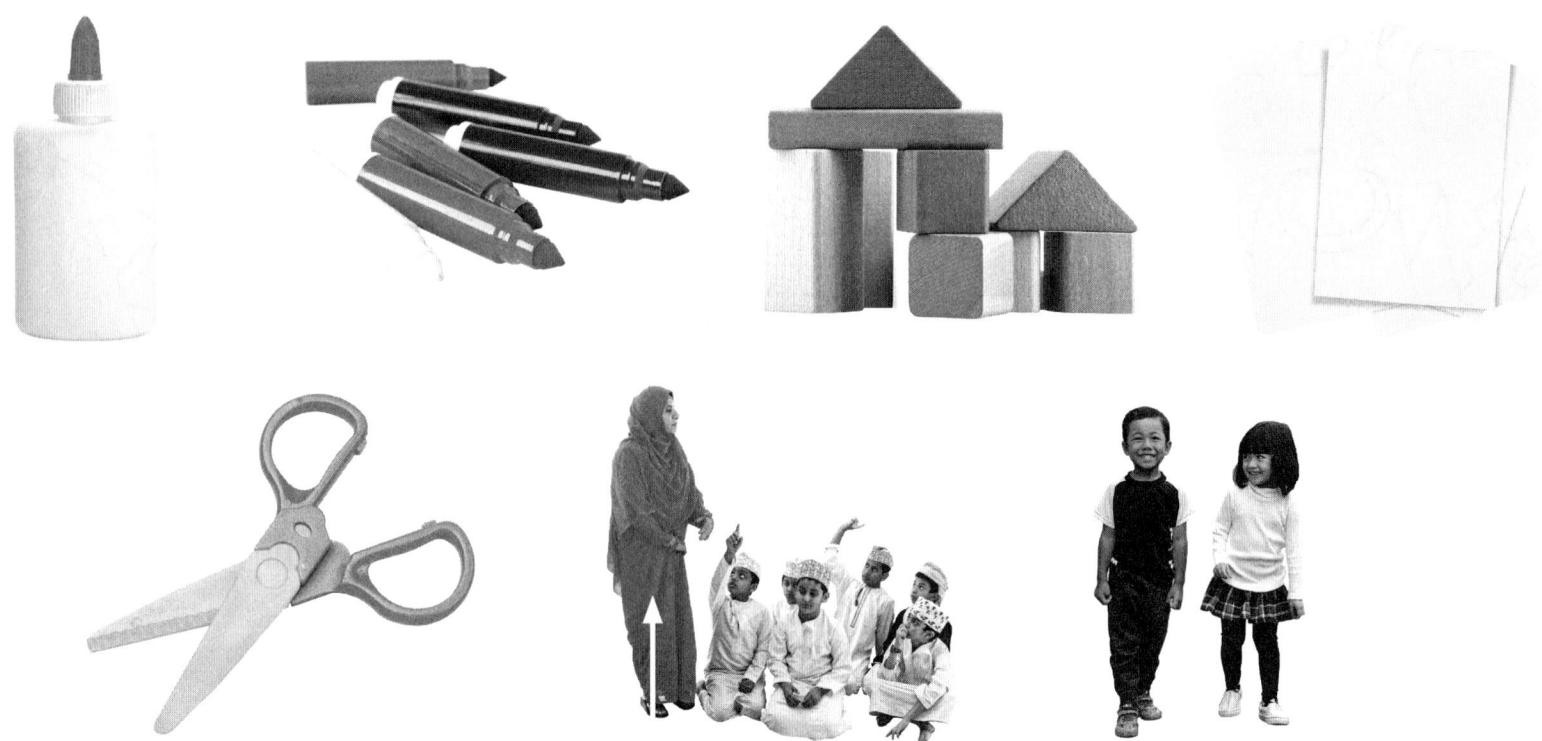

2 Point and say.

NEW WORDS: *blocks, friend, teacher; glue, markers, paper, scissors*

1 Draw your family and friends. Then point and say.

STRUCTURE: *Who's this? He's my grandpa. She's my friend.*

5

1 TR: 1.2 Circle. Then listen, sing, and point.

2 Look and circle ✔ or ✘.

VALUE Be neat in the classroom.

1 ✔ ✘

2 ✔ ✘

3 ✔ ✘

1 TR: 1.3 Listen and say.

beaver

panda

2 Trace.

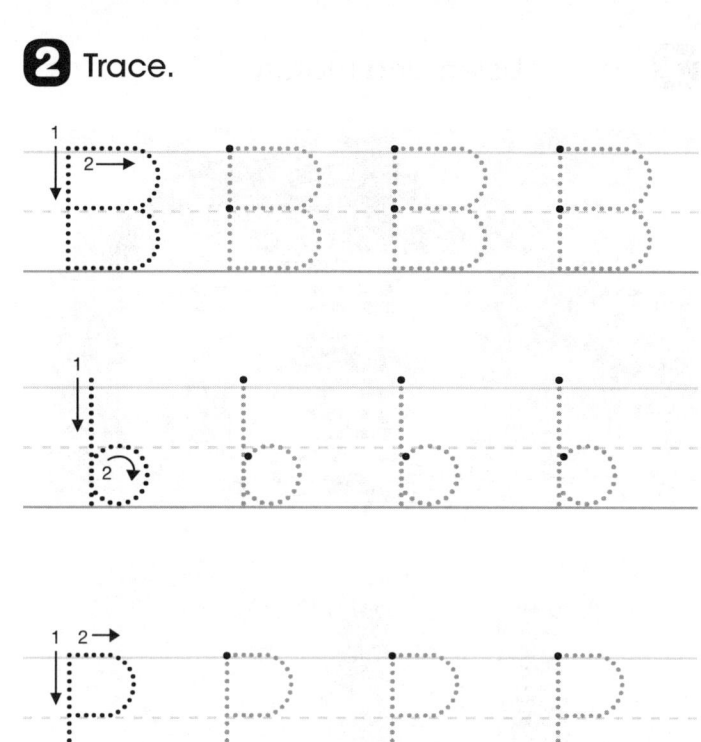

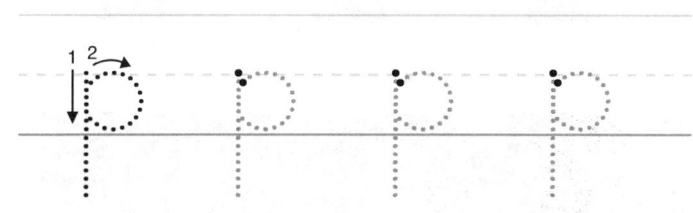

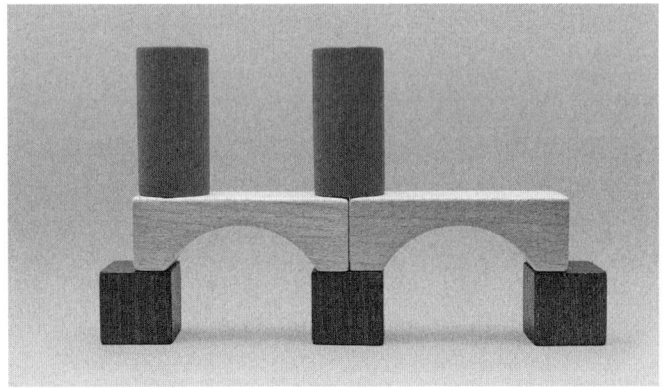

1 TR: 1.5 Listen and point. Then say and color.

REVIEW: **NEW WORDS**: *blocks, friend, teacher; glue, markers, paper, scissors*
STRUCTURE: *Who's this? He's my grandpa. She's my friend.*

Are You Happy?

1 TR: 2.1 Listen. Circle ✔ or ✘.

1 (✔) ✘   2 ✔ ✘   3 ✔ ✘   4 ✔ ✘

5 ✔ ✘   6 ✔ ✘   7 ✔ ✘

2 Point and say.

NEW WORDS: *angry, excited, happy, hungry, sad, sleepy, thirsty*

1 Draw you. Then point and say.

STRUCTURE: *Are you happy? Yes, I am. Are you sad? No, I'm not.*

1 TR: 2.2 Listen and circle. Then listen, sing, and point.

2 Look and circle ✔ or ✘.

VALUE   Get a good night's sleep.

1 ✔ ✘

2 ✔ ✘

3 ✔ ✘

1 TR: 2.3 Listen and say.

duck

tiger

2 Trace.

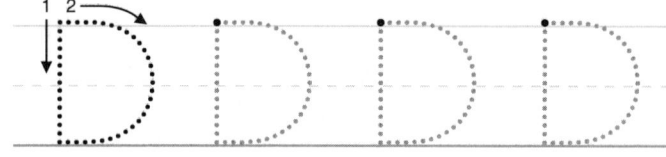

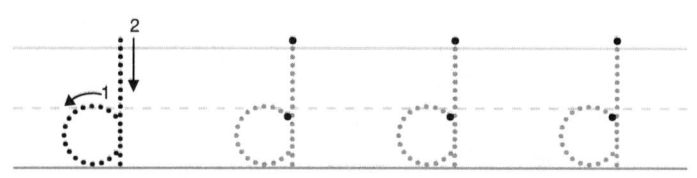

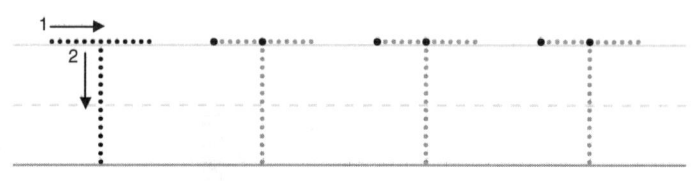

1 TR: 2.4 Listen and match. Then color your favorite.

1 2 3 4

VIDEO: SC: 4 *(optional)* **Content Words:** *loud, music, quiet*

1 Play and say.

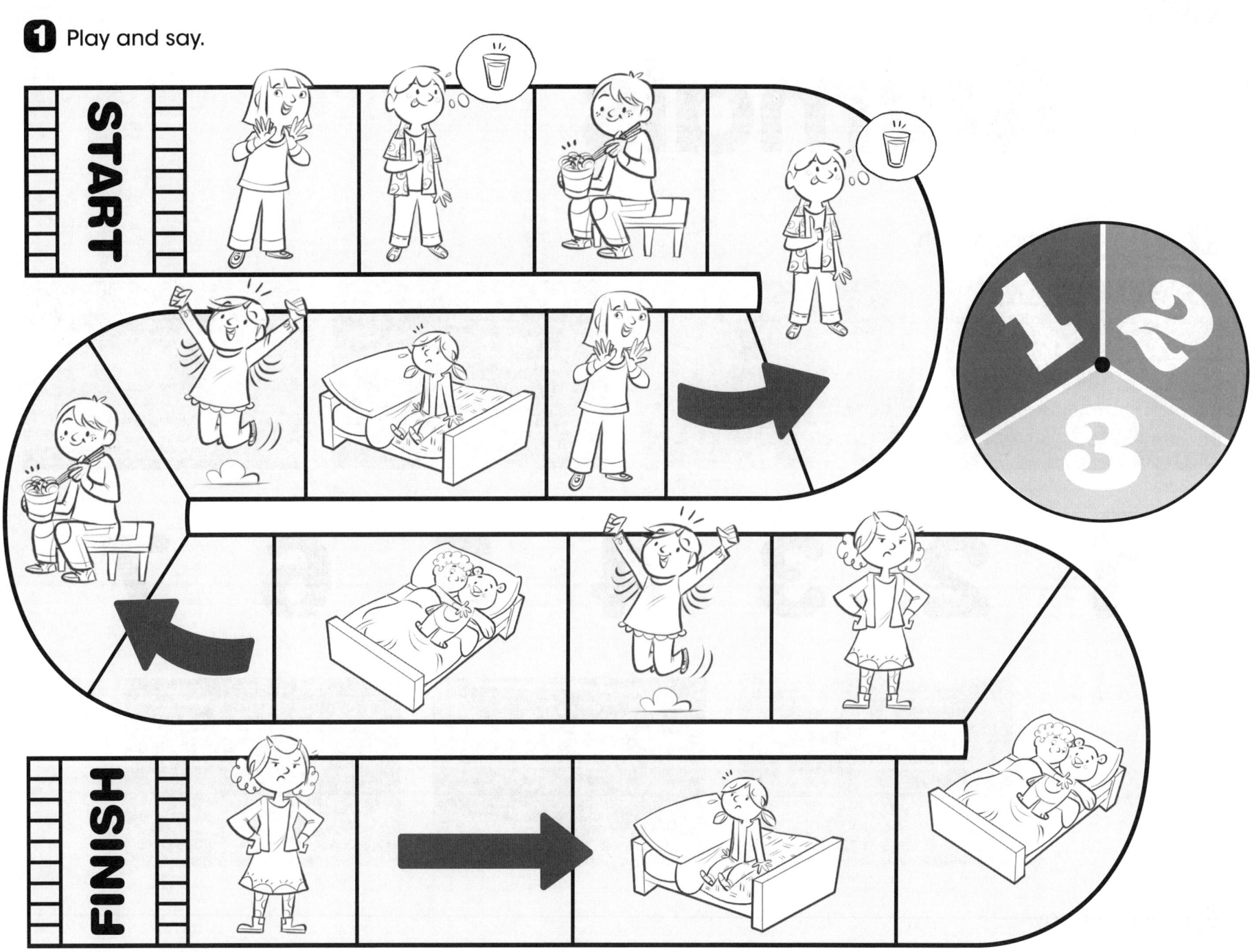

REVIEW: **NEW WORDS**: *angry, excited, happy, hungry, sad, sleepy, thirsty*
STRUCTURE: *Are you happy? Yes, I am. Are you sad? No, I'm not.*

15

3 Animals

1 TR: 3.1 Listen and match.

1   2   3   4   5   6   7

2 Point and say.

16   **NEW WORDS:** *bat, bear, duck, fox, owl, rabbit, snake*

1 Match. Then ask and answer.

1 TR: 3.2 Listen and color. Then listen, sing, and point.

2 Look and circle ✔ or ✗.

VALUE   Be curious about animals.

1 ✔ ✗

2 ✔ ✗

3 ✔ ✗

1 TR: **3.3** Listen and say.

seal

zebra

2 Trace.

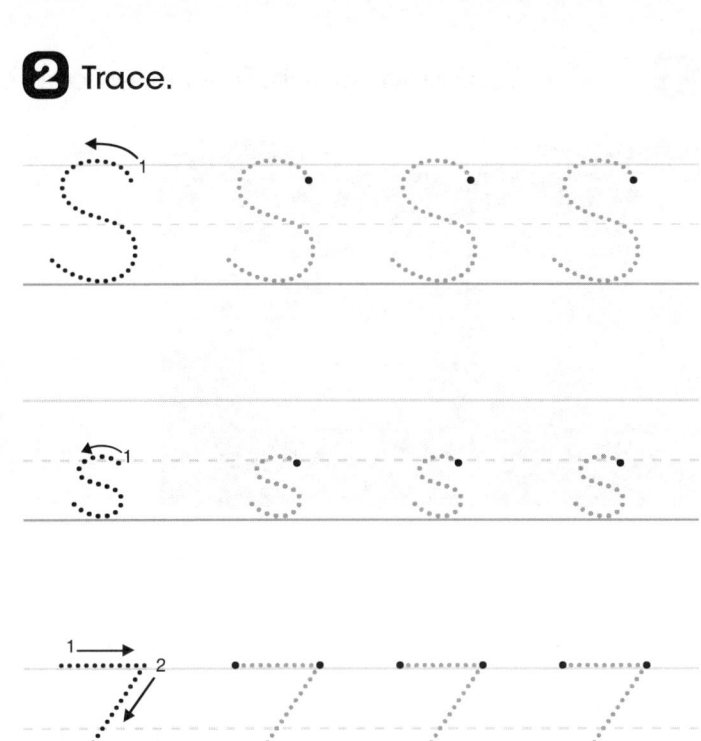

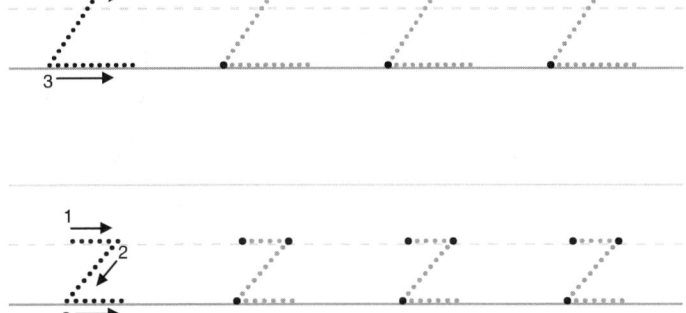

1 TR: 3.4 Look and match. Then listen and check.

VIDEO: SC: 6 *(optional)* **Content Words:** *day, night*

1 Find and color. Then ask and answer.

REVIEW: **NEW WORDS**: *bat, bear, duck, fox, owl, rabbit, snake*
STRUCTURE: *What is it? It's an owl. What are they? They're bears.*

1 TR: 4.1 Listen and point.

2 Point and say.

NEW WORDS: *boots, coat, dress, pants, scarf, skirt, sweater*

1 Draw and color. Then match and say.

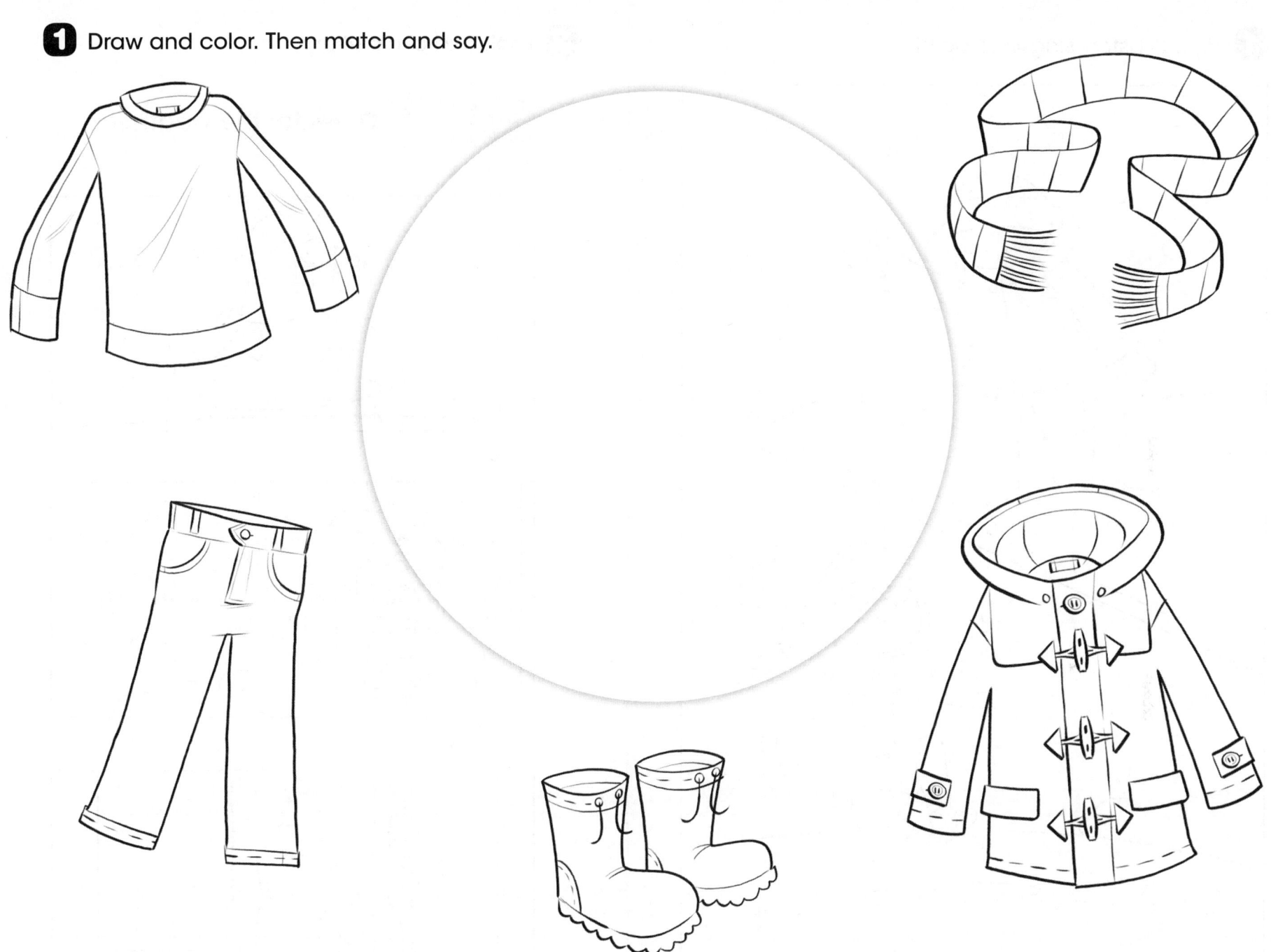

1 TR: 4.2 Listen, sing, and point.

2 Look and circle ✔ or ✘.

VALUE Dress for the weather.

1 ✔ ✘

2 ✔ ✘

3 ✔ ✘

1 TR: 4.3 Listen and say.

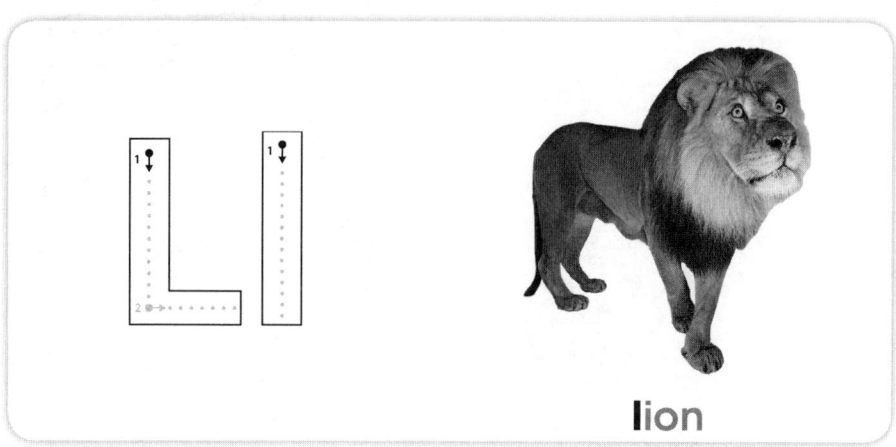

lion

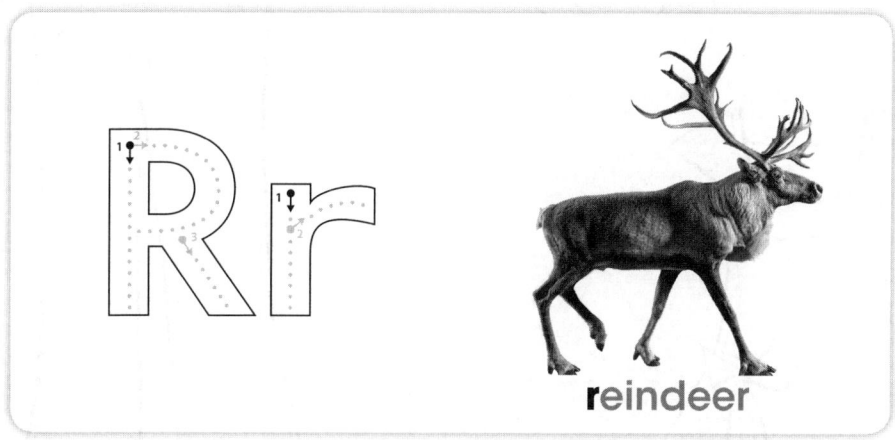

reindeer

2 Trace.

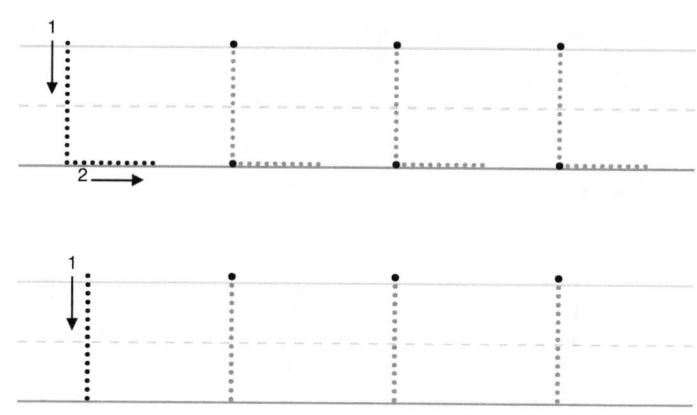

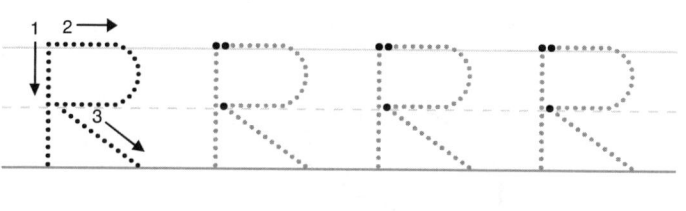

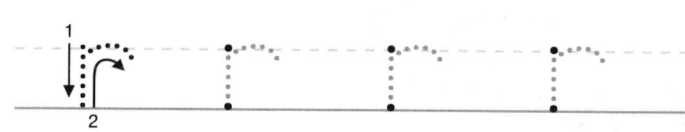

1 TR: 4.4 Listen and match.

VIDEO: SC: 8 *(optional)* **Content Words:** *cotton, plant, silk, worm*

1 Color. Play and say.

REVIEW: **NEW WORDS**: *boots, coat, dress, pants, scarf, skirt, sweater*
STRUCTURE: *This is my sweater. These are my pants.*

5 I Can Jump!

1 TR: 5.1 Listen. Circle ✔ or ✘.

1 ✔ ✘

2 ✔ ✘

3 ✔ ✘

4 ✔ ✘

5 ✔ ✘

6 ✔ ✘

7 ✔ ✘

2 Point and say.

28   **NEW WORDS:** *crawl, dance, hop, jump, run, turn around, walk*

1 Do and say.

1 TR: 5.2 Listen and point. Then sing and do.

2 Look and circle ✔ or ✘.

VALUE   Play outside.

1 ✔ ✘

2 ✔ ✘

3 ✔ ✘

1 TR: 5.3 Listen and say.

monkey

numbat

2 Trace.

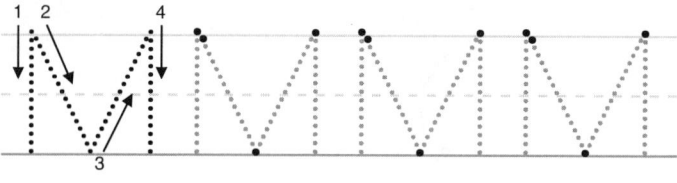

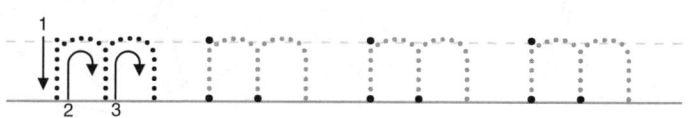

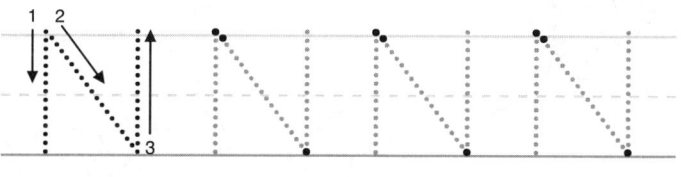

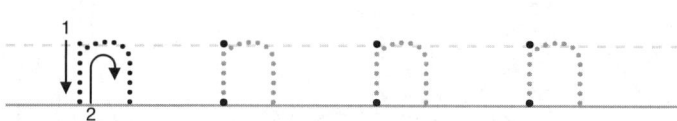

1 TR: 5.4 Listen and color.

VIDEO: SC: 10 (optional) **Content Words:** *climb, hopscotch, playground*

1 What can you do? Color, say, and do.

1 TR: 6.1 Listen and point.

2 TR: 6.2 Listen and draw.

1

2

3

1 TR: 6.3 Listen. Then draw and color. Say.

STRUCTURE: *He has brown eyes. She has long hair.*

1 TR: 6.4 Listen and color. Then sing and point.

2 Look and circle ✔ or ✗.

VALUE Say nice things.

1 ✔ ✗

2 ✔ ✗

3 ✔ ✗

1 TR: 6.5 Listen and say.

gorilla

hippo

2 Trace.

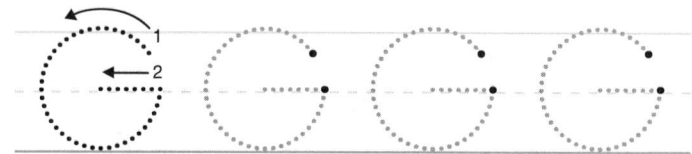

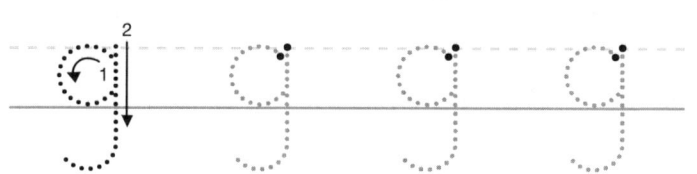

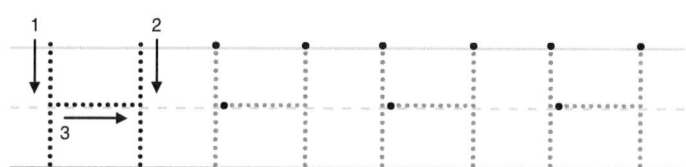

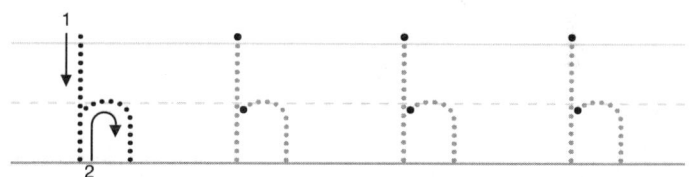

1 Look and match.

VIDEO: SC: 12 *(optional)*   **Content Words:** *hear, smell, taste, the senses*

1 Draw, color, and say.

REVIEW: NEW WORDS: *ears, eyes, face, hair, mouth, nose; long, short*
STRUCTURE: *He has brown eyes. She has long hair.*

7 My Things

1 TR: 7.1 Listen and match.

1 2 3 4 5 6 7

2 Point and say.

NEW WORDS: *bike, dinosaur, kite, puzzle, robot, scooter, tablet*

1 Draw one toy. Ask and answer.

1 TR: 7.2 Listen and circle. Then sing and point.

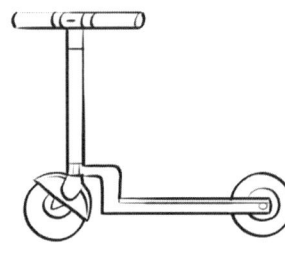

2 Look and circle ✔ or ✘.

VALUE   Take turns.

1 ✔ ✘

2 ✔ ✘

3 ✔ ✘

1 TR: 7.3 Listen and say.

camel

quail

2 Trace.

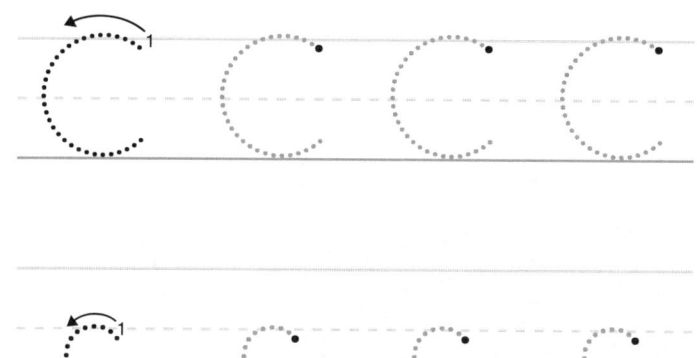

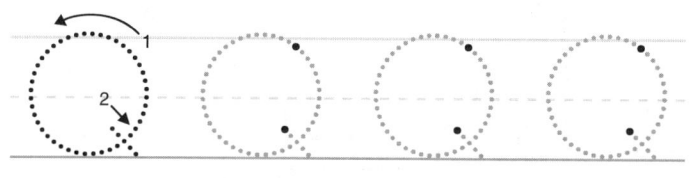

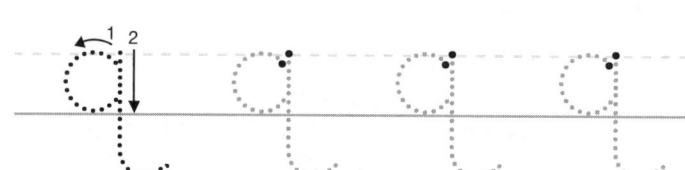

1 Color and count.

VIDEO: SC: 14 *(optional)* **Content Words:** *ground, neck, skeleton, tail*

1 Color. Ask and answer.

REVIEW: NEW WORDS: *bike, dinosaur, kite, puzzle, robot, scooter, tablet*
STRUCTURE: *Is this your kite? Yes, it is./No, it isn't.*

45

8 Babies

1 TR: 8.1 Listen and match.

2 TR: 8.2 Listen and point. Then say.

NEW WORDS: *baby, calf, chick, kitten, lamb, puppy; big, small*

1 TR: 8.3 Listen and point. Then say.

STRUCTURE: *There's one cow. There are two calves.*

1 TR: 8.4 Listen and point. Then color.

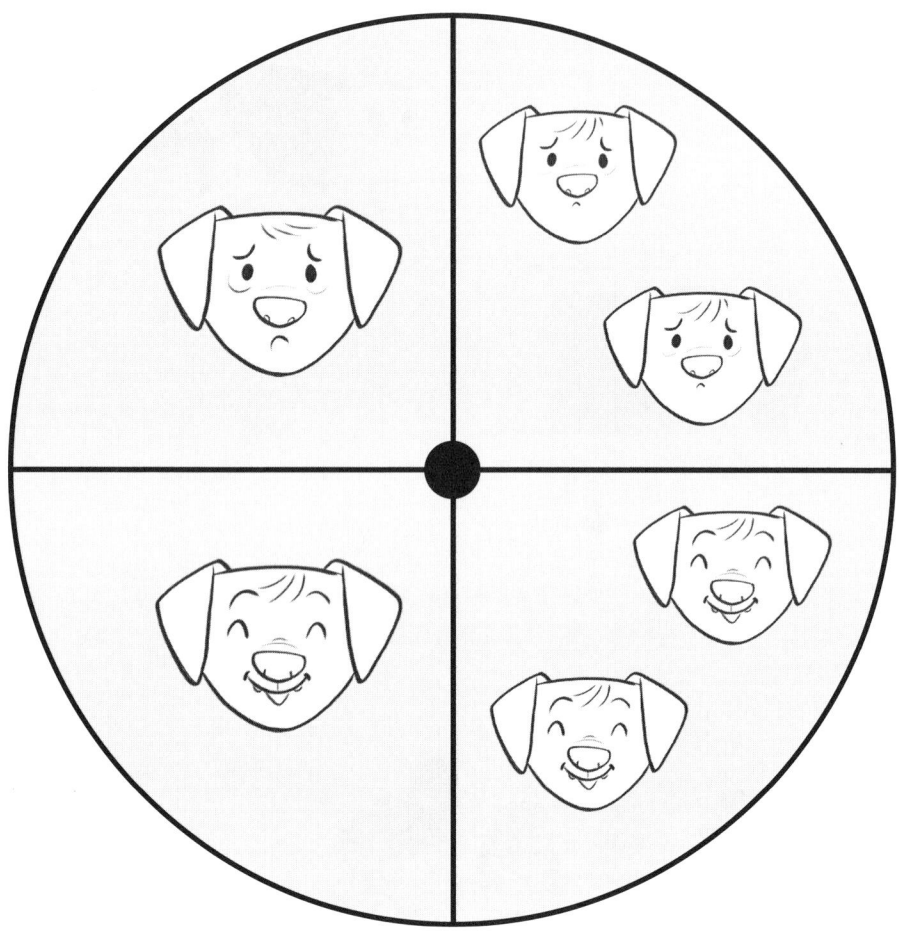

2 Look and circle ✔ or ✘.

VALUE   Be kind.

1 ✔ ✘

2 ✔ ✘

3 ✔ ✘

1 TR: 8.5 Listen and say.

kangaroo

fox

2 Trace.

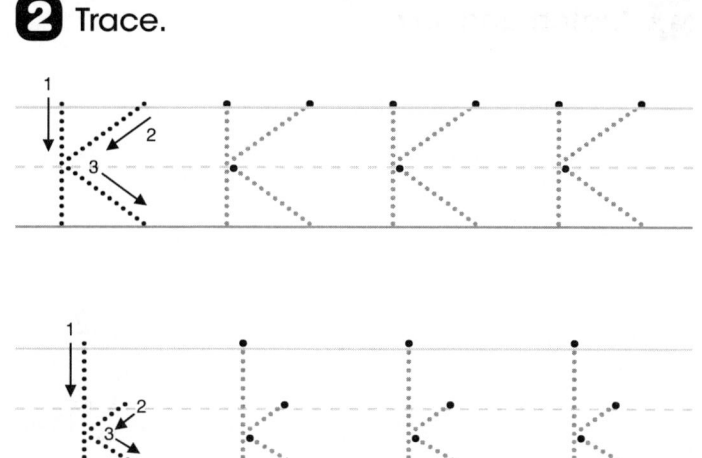

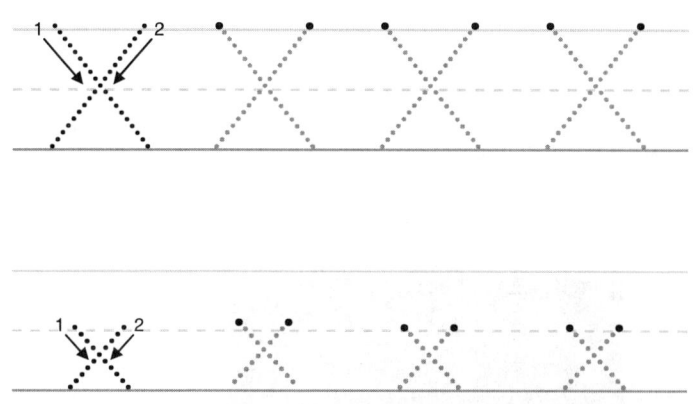

1 Match and say.

VIDEO: SC: 16 *(optional)*   **Content Words:** *ant, egg, ostrich*

1 Color and say.

REVIEW: **NEW WORDS**: *baby, calf, chick, kitten, lamb, puppy; big, small*
STRUCTURE: *There's one cow. There are two calves.*

What's for Dinner?

1 TR: 9.1 Listen. Circle ✔ or ✘.

1 ✔ ✘ 2 ✔ ✘ 3 ✔ ✘ 4 ✔ ✘

5 ✔ ✘ 6 ✔ ✘ 7 ✔ ✘ 8 ✔ ✘

2 Point and say.

NEW WORDS: *beans, bread, chicken, dinner, fish, noodles, rice, salad*

1 TR: 9.2 Listen and match. Then say.

1

2

3

4

5

6

STRUCTURE: *What do you want? I want chicken, please.*

53

1
TR: 9.3 Listen and circle. Then color and sing.

2
Look and circle ✔ or ✘.

VALUE Help in the kitchen.

1 ✔ ✘

2 ✔ ✘

3 ✔ ✘

1 TR: 9.4 Listen and say.

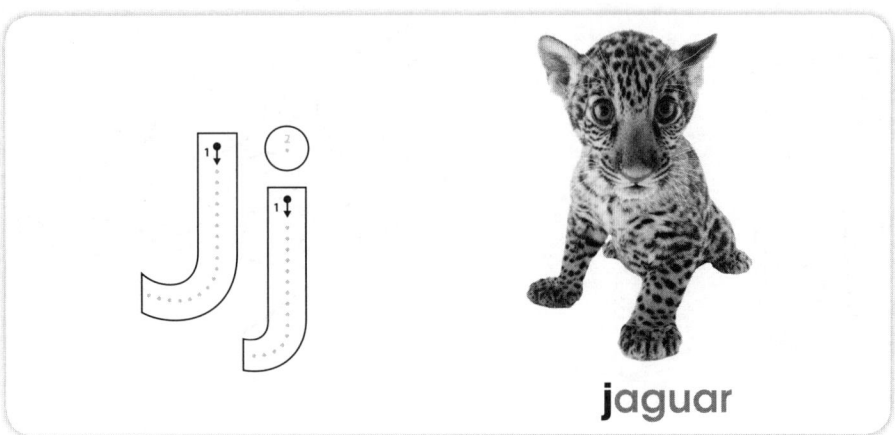

jaguar

yak

2 Trace.

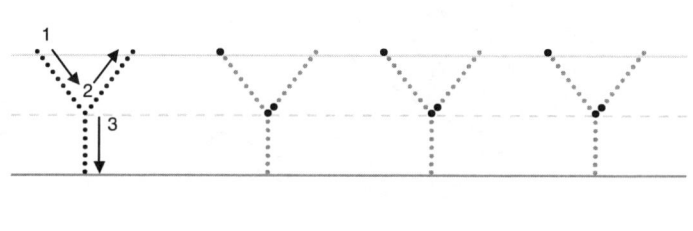

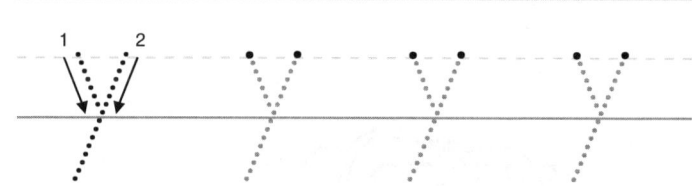

1 TR: 9.5 Let's make soup! Listen and circle.

1 What's for dinner? Draw.

REVIEW: **NEW WORDS**: *beans, bread, chicken, dinner, fish, noodles, rice, salad*
STRUCTURE: *What do you want? I want chicken, please.*

57

10 Bugs

1 TR: 10.1 Listen and match.

1 2 3 4 5 6 7

2 Look and say.

NEW WORDS: *ant, bee, butterfly, caterpillar, ladybug, snail, spider*

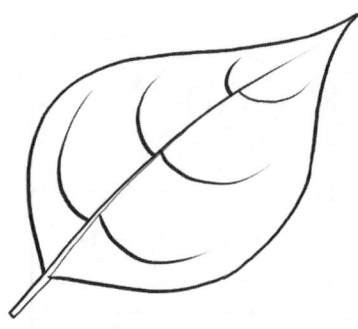

STRUCTURE: *Where's the caterpillar? It's on an apple.*

1 TR: 10.3 Listen and draw. Then sing and point.

2 Look and circle ✔ or ✗.

VALUE   Be good to nature.

1 ✔ ✗

2 ✔ ✗

3 ✔ ✗

1 TR: 10.4 Listen and say.

fish

vulture

wolf

2 Trace.

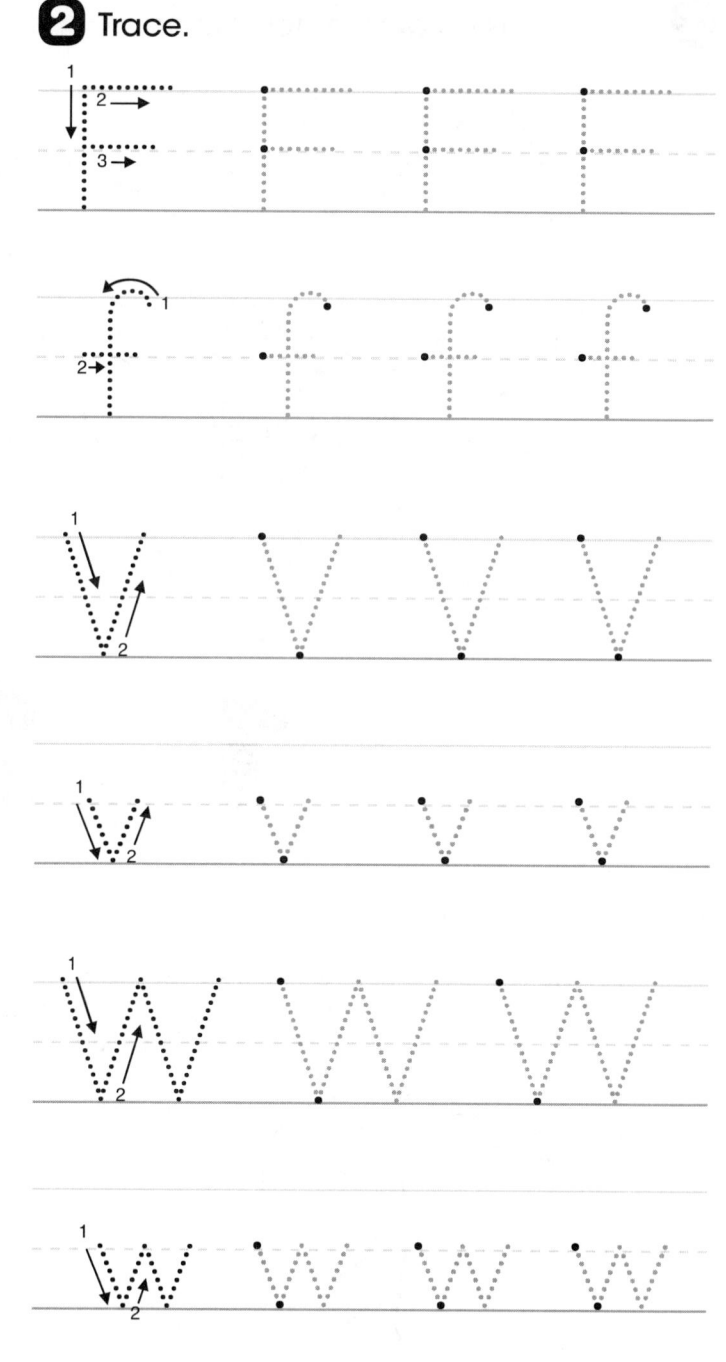

1 Listen and match. Color.

VIDEO: SC: 20 *(optional)*   Content Word: *pupa*

1 Look and say. Find. Then color.

REVIEW: **NEW WORDS:** *ant, bee, butterfly, caterpillar, ladybug, snail, spider*
STRUCTURE: *Where's the caterpillar? It's on an apple.*

63

BERLITZ MID-LEVEL TEST

Please do not open

Writing score: _____ */50*   *Speaking score:* _____ */50*

Name: _____

Listen and circle. (6 points)

Example:

1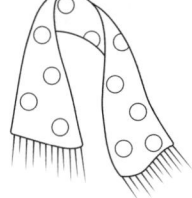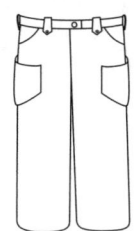

2

3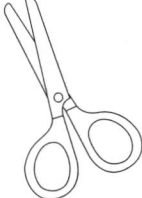

Listen and draw. (6 points)

4

5

Listen. Circle ✔ or ✘. (8 points)

Example:  ✔

✘

6  ✔ ✘   **7**  ✔ ✘   **8**  ✔ ✘   **9**  ✔ ✘

Circle the small letters. (8 points)

10  B   b   d   p   d   b   b

11  M   n   m   w   n   w   m

Trace the small letter. Then write 4 big letters. (10 points)

12 t

13 d

Listen and circle. (8 points)

Example:

14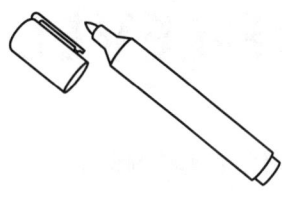

16

15

17

18 Write your full name. (4 points)

BERLITZ END-OF-LEVEL TEST

Please do not open

Writing score: _____ / 50   Speaking score: _____ / 50

Name: _____

Listen and circle. **(6 points)**

Example:

 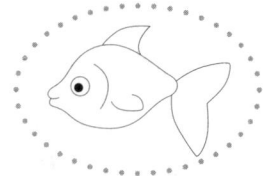 

Draw and color. **(8 points)**

1

4

2

5

3

Listen. Circle ✔ or ✗. (8 points)

Example:

✔

✗

6 ✔ ✗

7 ✔ ✗

8 ✔ ✗

9 ✔ ✗

Circle the big letters. (8 points)

10 f   E   T   F   E   F   E

11 v   V   V   W   M   W   V

Trace the big letter. Then write 4 small letters. (10 points)

12 J

13 Y

Listen and circle. (8 points)

Example:

 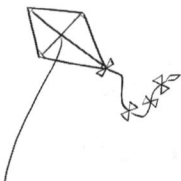

14

16

15

17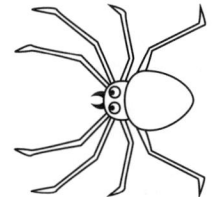

18 Circle the animals starting with C. (2 points)

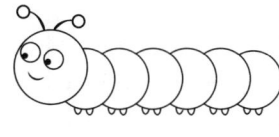   

Unit 3 Color and say.

Unit 4 Color and say.

Unit 5 Color and say.

Unit 6 Draw, color, and say.

Color and say.

CREDITS